True Story

Also by Randy Blasing

POETRY

*A Change of Heart*
*Sweet Crude*
*Choice Words: Poems 1970-2005*
*Second Home*
*Graphic Scenes*
*The Double House of Life*
*The Particles*
*To Continue*
*Light Years*

SELECTED TRANSLATIONS (with Mutlu Konuk)

*Poems of Nazim Hikmet*
*Human Landscapes from My Country:*
   *An Epic Novel in Verse by Nazim Hikmet*
*Letters to Taranta-Babu: A Poem by Nazim Hikmet*

# TRUE STORY

### POEMS

## Randy Blasing

Copper Beech Press
Providence

Grateful acknowledgment is made to the editors of
*The Yale Review*, which first published "Storm Warning."

Cover painting: *Sunset at Cannon Point, Dalyan, Turkey,
After a Photograph by Ezra Blasing.*
© 2020 by K.L. Martel

Author photograph © 2019
by the Community College of Rhode Island

Copyright © 2020 by Randy Blasing

All rights reserved.
For information, address the publisher:
Copper Beech Press
Post Office Box 2578
Providence, Rhode Island 02906

Library of Congress Control Number: 2020915085

ISBN: 978-1-952521-41-6

Publisher's Cataloging-In-Publication Data
(Prepared by The Donohue Group, Inc.)

Names: Blasing, Randy, author.
Title: True story : poems / by Randy Blasing.
Description: First edition. | Providence, [Rhode Island] : Copper Beech Press, [2020] |
   "Storm Warning" previously published in the Yale Review.
Identifiers: ISBN 9781952521416
Subjects: LCSH: Blasing, Randy--Poetry. | American poetry.
Classification: LCC PS3552.L38 T78 2020 | DDC 811/.54--dc23

Set in Adobe Garamond Pro
Printed by Stillwater River Publications
Manufactured in the United States of America
First Edition

*for Kerri Lee*

*We make a dwelling in the evening air,
In which being there together is enough.*
                WALLACE STEVENS

CONTENTS

*I*

May Day  3
Preacher's Kid  4
Country Music  5
Last Light  6
Sweethearts  7
Double Crossing  8
The Localist  9
The Revisionist  10
First Return to My One-Time Second Home  11

*II*

On the Turquoise Trail at Seventy-Five  19
More Alive than Ever  21
Flight School  22
Night Life  23
Between the Lines  24
Ecclesiastes Rides Shotgun  25
Sundown  26
Sanctuary City  27
There Would Be Hell to Pay  30

*III*

Blackstone River Blues  35
After Long Silence  40
Oral Communication  41
Love Poem to My First Reader  42
Jack's Abby  43

Easter Monday   *44*
The White Crow   *45*
Rachmaninoff's "Lilacs"   *46*
Of Little Faith   *47*

*IV*

Seeing Double in New Mexico   *51*
My Father Contemplates His Hunting Fetish   *53*
Night Flight   *54*
B-17   *55*
Gladiolus: A History   *56*
Against Winter   *57*
Variable Cloudiness, Then Stars   *58*
Pursuing Happiness   *59*
End of Story   *62*

*V*

World War III   *65*

# I

MAY DAY

The bank says it's seventy-five this morning,
the average temperature in Paradise
(San Diego, Laguna Beach, La Jolla)
in my experience. The turquoise sky
draws a blank on clouds, & every last tree
I see went up in green leaves overnight,
destined though it is to alchemize
into gold & melt down, reverting
to lead in six months, its half-life accomplished.

I've lived a whole year for this day, half-dead
as I was a year ago at this time,
& dead as I would be on the first day
of summer then, when I returned to life
& started on my way back home to here,
the land of the living, from zombie country,
where my broken heart got cut out & patched
together with cowhide, which brings me up
to date: today I've died & gone to heaven.

# PREACHER'S KID

As usual your father was in church,
praying for you who had run off with me,
the day you called with the good news his first

grandkid (according to your sonogram)
would be a boy. "Praise the Lord!" he no sooner
shouted to his absent congregation,

weekday that it was, than he elaborated:
"The apple has a stem!" I always gave
thanks for your amazing grace when you tied

my cherry stem in knots with just your tongue,
but I never knew a "P.K." was a *handful,*
till childhood friends back home in Minnesota

brought me up to speed. After all, we rocked
our vows at last in Vegas, not in church,
tying the knot in the Valley of Fire.

COUNTRY MUSIC


It made their day, the Seniors who'd escaped
from elderly housing down the road & sat,
smoking, outside McDonald's Sunday morning
when you rolled up with me in your Mercedes
blacker than coffee, which got them all going.

Then, when you hopped out from behind the wheel
of your vintage automobile, they stepped
up their storytelling on finding you
so many years my junior, "vintage" myself,
& put their heads together, best they could,

under their straw hats. You'd clearly taken
a wrong turn somewhere, in their eyes, to end
up *there*, of all places, you who'd appeared
out of nowhere like a VIP,
a godsend to their old imaginations.

## LAST LIGHT

The sun gone down on the first summer day,
my second son stood showing his first car
to his two grandparents in the last light,
a sixteen-year-old with an M3 almost
his age who, the night suddenly too cool
to be cool, still dropped its top for the full
effect of its cinnamon heart in the dark,
which gave them pause, together with its quad
exhausts he revved like the end of the world.

His life their only ticket to the future
here on earth, their faces said they didn't like
their chances when they saw someone as young
as him behind the wheel of so much car,
whose grandfather he never knew found me,
for *my* first car, a slammed blue '56
Chevrolet Bel Air with dual exhausts
I left rumbling at the curb outside
of Kathy's house the night of my first kiss.

SWEETHEARTS

> *Boink I love you.*
> JOHN ASHBERY


All night I dreamed of Janice, my first crush:
the first thing every morning in eighth grade,
we traded smiles across our homeroom.

In rumpus rooms through the year, we slow-danced
to "Teen Angel," our cheeks glued together
with sweat, her pointy breasts aimed at my heart

& hitting it. On the last day of school,
she leaned back against the wall outside
of English, one leg bent so her raised knee

pushed up her pink sun-dress & sent it falling
between her legs, giving me an instant
erection in the hall. My dream of going

further only came true last night in bed
when she undressed from the waist down, legs tanned
all the way up, as far as I could see.

DOUBLE CROSSING

Mother goose marches her brood of five goslings
across the road between a pond & freshly

seeded grass, followed by her black-helmeted
gander hissing, left & right, like Darth Vader

under a warning sign: "Make Way for Ducklings"
(right spot, wrong bird). What matters, then, if not

whatever lies before my eyes in this,
the material world, vis-à-vis the other

world of spirits, which I have gone & seen
with my own eyes exists for real. I pledge

allegiance to both worlds—these geese the passing
traffic stopped dead for & let pass this day

in June, & that sphere of endless peace I died
last June to reach, no sooner delivered there

than still accorded my desire to see
things pass before my eyes again down here.

# THE LOCALIST

> *I'd like to be at McCoy Stadium*
> *watching a good game of baseball.*
> GALWAY KINNELL

Growing up in the early fifties, I saw
Willie Mays play centerfield for the Millers
in Minneapolis with Rance Pless,
Billy Gardner, & Wayne Terwilliger.

Out at Metropolitan Stadium
in the late fifties, I saw Carl Yastrzemski
star with his supporting cast of "Pumpsie"
Green, Jim Mahoney, & Jerry Zimmerman.

Tonight I sat still for the final game
of my fiftieth season at McCoy,
but when a shaky *V* of Canada geese
arrowed south out of left field, sunset smeared

across the threadbare sky above Pawtucket,
I suddenly recalled those unknown names
destined, like mine, to vanish in the dust,
career minor-leaguers untouched by fame.

# THE REVISIONIST

*Scrutinize your work with a fine-toothed comb.*
  MY HOROSCOPE

"*Revise, revise, revise,*" Elizabeth
Bishop heard songbirds in Maine insist
to her ear after her friend Cal's demise

two years before her own. My end clearly
in sight, each night I do as my stars ask,
setting things right before my time runs out.

Second thoughts? By my lights, second chances!
I burn the midnight oil against the dark
& cold, endless winter coming on

as it must, & bring to light my last words
I must live with & give the final say,
not for now but forever (don't I wish).

# FIRST RETURN TO MY ONE-TIME SECOND HOME

*1. Cesme Peninsula*

I must have died again & gone to heaven
again, back at the same exact beach
in Turkey where, upwards now of fifty

summers ago, I swam in salt water
(coming from the Land of 10,000 Lakes
as I was) for the first time in my life,

the sea pale emerald but diamond-clear
to this day, still lying down at my feet
as good as gold. A blown-up golden swan

steamed past, powered by someone's dad; my younger
son dived for a baby cloth-of-gold cone
as small as it was rare. Those days were golden,

slipping away like the last grains of sand
in my hourglass, but meanwhile life continued
along the water's edge: a boy gone bald

from chemo took the shoreline in stride;
a pregnant woman in a black bikini,
a two-master inked on her belly, entered

the sea at full sail; & the three youngest
of an old guy's four wives, all covered head
to foot by wetsuits underneath their long

dresses, giggled leaving land, one preserving
her life by flying an orange pool noodle
under clouds so close that I could taste them.

*2. Sea Spa*

Before taking the waters of the clear-
as-day, blue-green-as-verdigris Aegean,
you & I toasted high noon together

with amber bottles of *Weissbier,* Erdinger's
gold elixir I first tasted smuggled me
flying Economy on Lufthansa

yesterday. A year ago today,
an ambulance flew me to rehab after
I'd come back to life four times & then passed
fourteen days flat in bed. You followed me

down my long road back from the Other Side
to this Turkish seaside, where every last
day of my recovery I had dreamed
of landing one more time, alive & well.

3. His Brother's Keeper

Volcanic clouds looming on the horizon
today, a regatta of sailboats lit
up the bay, a flock of white butterflies
catching their breath mid-migratory flight

between seasons. Taking the plunge with me,
you licked your lips, proclaiming the sea tasted
like oysters, clean & salty, & like the past,
the mountains lost their black mood & assumed

a rosy glow. My older son appeared
like a mirage on this Turkish beach I'd called
home fifteen summers, & took our boy swimming
in open sea off Dalyan, where I taught him

to swim at five. Now, at thirty-something,
he made his brother half his age at home.

4. *Storm Warning*

> *Perhaps the system*
> *Calls for spirits.*
> JAMES MERRILL

Last night my son celebrated his marriage,
descending with his Turkish bride from a green
mid-century Bel Air to U2's "All
I Want Is You" & dancing under stars

installed, as if for them, where horses roamed
a ranch all bushy olive trees in Urla,
home of the poet George Seferis I once
visited by way of paying him homage.

Greeks came bearing gifts from across the water:
songs inspired, a poet's son from Chios
announced in English, plucking them from his strings,
by a Greek translation of Nazim Hikmet's

quatrain to his wife from Bursa Prison
"The most beautiful sea hasn't been crossed yet"
(my translation, as it happened, but who knew).
Prohibition knocking on the door now,

an amber river of Johnnie Black freely
flowed through the night, till a SWAT team shut down
—what—the last Turkish wedding to serve spirits?
I saw history made in the name of love.

II

# ON THE TURQUOISE TRAIL AT SEVENTY-FIVE

*1. 4:20 PM on Route 66*

My only habit is remembering:
frothy white clouds churning into the picture
behind Sandia Peak dead-ahead threatened
to spill over its stony face, stoned
as it appeared, seeing how high it was.
I just looked forward to a cold Blue Moon,
after spending the day with you to get
outfitted as the cowboy I still wanted

to be: beads the pale turquoise of stone-washed
Levi's at my throat; a Texas Rangers star
pinned on my chest; & at my waist a Zuni
buckle all inlays & geometry.
When I go you-know-where, these things will keep
alive this long-lost day in Albuquerque,
& I will go down in your memory
as the cowboy I never got to be.

*2. High Noon on Americas Parkway*

Clouds mushroom into view around the ragged
edges of the turquoise sky that inspired
the latest New Mexico plates. A sky-
rocketing vapor trail fizzles out
in squiggles where it launched. Yesterday a red-
tail cruised the thermals up & down the trail
you blazed to Santa Fe in our Hertz Versa
below one after another black mesa.

I've felt at home here over forty years,
ever since the summer when, "midway
through my life," I plunged into an inferno,
driving cross-country, & followed my heart
to Taos, where I found the words so far
for "West," my Bicentennial travel log.
Back five years to the good, I've turned the page
all thanks to you, earth angel half my age.

## MORE ALIVE THAN EVER

I see clouds differently now that I've learned
from my experience they're home to heaven
after all, the "Happy Hunting Ground"
in the sky that I believed in as a kid

in Minnesota, where the Chippewas
(invisible, everyhere I looked) seized
my Presbyterian imagination
mainly because, in their cosmology,

my bird dog, Blackie, would ascend to heaven
along with me; I couldn't fathom life
without her then, eternal or otherwise..
In time, of course, I lapsed in my belief,

until last summer when one last Code Blue
launched me through clouds I came out on top of,
& I found peace while dying, in my heart
of hearts, to find myself back here below.

# FLIGHT SCHOOL

In 1951, when he turned forty,
my father used the GI Bill, enrolling
in flying lessons on Uncle Sam's dime.

Sunday mornings when I was eight, he woke
at six & drove me out to Flying Cloud
in Shakopee. My mother still asleep

in our Golden Valley ranch, I curled up
in the back seat of his maroon Cessna
& slept myself, while he earned hours toward

his private license with an eye to cutting
down on the time he spent driving to sell
thread & buttons to his territory.

Taking flight as I am, did I perversely
get something by osmosis from those lessons,
aloft now on the wings of my mother tongue?

## NIGHT LIFE

A dimpled white spider above the door
of my space-gray 335 tonight
hung over my head like the evening star
I saw break through the overcast the first

of October, the month deer season opened
when I was still a kid in Minnesota
& waited for my father to bring home
a doe or buck slung across his right fender

late one Sunday night in ashen November,
which found my little family of three
sitting down, in time, to a venison
dinner & feasting on the game my father

hunted down & my mother cooked in wine
too sweet to drink—such suppertimes together
made me the different animal I am
who can still taste the honey of those nights.

## BETWEEN THE LINES

> *Writing is exciting*
> *and baseball is like writing.*
> *You can never tell with either*
> *how it will go*
> *or what you will do . . .*
>     MARIANNE MOORE

October afternoons throughout the fifties
I ran home after school to catch the final
innings of a World Series game—in black

& white, of course, & mainly in New York—
in time to watch the shadows fall across
home plate & come between, say, Whitey Ford

& Jackie Robinson. Eventually,
they brought the curtain down on one more season
& ushered in another Minnesota

winter of practicing my level swing
in the living-room mirror, where I dug
into the wall-to-wall under my feet

& wore a hole in it. Without a big-league
home team to live & die by, I still fell
for baseball—my first love, before words even.

# ECCLESIASTES RIDES SHOTGUN

*for Ezra*

Here in October the lackluster green
of trees in September gives way to gold,
reminding me whatever is is precious,
considering it's all short-lived as long

as it's under the sun, my son & I
in his convertible included, top
down on the first day of Indian summer,
only a week away from his driver's test,

when he'll at last get his passport to life
without me & barrel, lead foot & all,
into tomorrow down whatever road
he happens to choose, happenstance being

everything, as when it happens this weather
is perfect for watching leaves turn together.

# SUNDOWN

>  *(Providence, 1970)*

*You didn't find God, you remembered him,*
you told me once, revising what I took
to be the bottom line of my last book.

*Be kind & believe,* my saintly old
Nana from Stavanger reminded me
time & again. For some reason, the time

she never called me on my passing off
my pre-born son's abortion as a mis-
carriage returned to me. She sat there staring

out the window by herself in silence,
as the light failed & left her in the dark
of my East Side apartment on Hope Street.

## SANCTUARY CITY

*1. "Family Needs $"*

So read the scrawled-on cardboard a panhandler
brandished at the stoplight at Benefit
Street, his usual Station of the Cross

along the road to the East Side, where those
blessed—if not with fortunes, at least good fortune—
have staked out the high ground (the hill, in fact,

George Washington claimed for his HQ once
upon a time), but the car in front of me
didn't go on green because the driver

handed the poor guy a fistful of crumpled-
up dollars extracted from wherever then
& there. When they slipped through his icy fingers,

though, they all scattered to the four winds,
& he gave chase as they blew across the street
into moving traffic like dead leaves, but green.

2. "New Arrivals in the U.S."

So said the cardboard sign displayed by one
big happy family caught in the rain
outside Whole Foods but stationed on the wrong
side (the passenger's) of passing cars whose
drivers couldn't extend them handouts from
tonight, though mom, dad, & the kids all grinned
from ear to ear while waving furiously,
hands working in synch with my wiper blades.

When my Norwegian grandmother arrived,
she found her way from Ellis Island as far
west as North Dakota, where she signed on
as kitchen help for families whose waves
of grain went on forever, like the ocean
she'd crossed at eighteen in 1900
to peel potatoes, but she understood
that she was free to eat the skins, & did.

3. *"Welcome, Refugees!"*

So went the poster covering the door
of a store selling this & that or odds
& ends on aptly named Hope Street. A black-

&-white sketch of one such refugee
—eyes sunken, scraggly beard, his hair a mess,
face gaunt—blocked the doorway with his haunted look.

I didn't get what I noticed next: a kid
tucked into his jacket peered out of it
a carbon copy of him, down to (yes!)

the beard. Was this a Middle Eastern version
of Russian nesting dolls, a refugee
inside a refugee, et cetera,

or victim upon victim of whomever
into eternity, *ad infinitum,*
fathers begetting their own hopelessness?

# THERE WOULD BE HELL TO PAY

*1. The National Anthem at the Car Show*

When it came on the loudspeaker instead
of fifties rock out in the parking lot

of Stop & Shop, everybody stood
at attention, right hands as close to their hearts

as their cars were. I looked up for the flag
but saw it only flew in their minds' eyes.

The early evening gave me chills, late summer
as it was, when I happened on two cars

my father dickered for & bought my mom
(her '51 red Sunliner that carted

my whole team to our ball game once, top down)
& me (my '56 turquoise Bel Air,

the "tank" that took out the black Mercedes
I hit on ice). The Beach Boys closed the show,

transporting me to '63—the year
I turned twenty & lost my father soon

after they wasted JFK. The country
I knew & loved would never feel the same.

2. Sixties Generation

I still remember sitting home & waiting
forever for my parents to return

from voting. They'd booked down to Noble School
together after work, intent (good-natured

as they were) on canceling out each other's vote
—my father a life-long Republican,

my mother still a Democrat—as they'd done
in every last Presidential election,

but this year it took them all night to battle
crowds waiting in line for voting booths,

where their Mutually Assured Destruction went
as planned again. The morning-after told

the story. As they'd gone, so had the nation—
a Mexican standoff (till one side stood down).

Three Novembers later, they saw their paper
ballots shot full of holes, a waste of time,

the powers-that-be out of their control.
When my time came to vote, I would stay home.

# III

# BLACKSTONE RIVER BLUES

> *... the enchainment of past and future*
> *Woven in the weakness of the changing body ...*
>               T. S. ELIOT

*1. Live Wire*

"Rough Road Ahead," warns the new yellow sign
on the Blackstone River Bikeway I've traversed
on foot a good two decades. It's about time:

last year I almost came to a dead stop
on it when I ran out of breath, my heart
failing big time. Yet following this path

had opened my heart to getting patched up
& letting me catch my breath again here
today, when I breathe deep like someone dying
of thirst inhaling a glass of ice water,

freezing air flooding my veins as if
ice water ran through them, cool customer
that I am now, still running for my life,
come-what-may down the old road ahead.

2. *Nine Inch Nails*

You always did get me "closer to God,"
in the words of their song, but when I died
& prayed to you both together to rise
from the dead, & did, their figure of speech

told the literal truth. I came back to life,
via heaven & the peace that truly
passed understanding, to the path I'd always
taken. Here in my turquoise windbreaker

from Santa Fe, designed to keep at bay
the elements, I walk on fallen leaves
again today, gold back under my feet,

but now a true believer in this world
& the next, up to my neck in the blue
of where one ends & the other begins.

*3. Sex Life*

No sooner had the bleached limbs of a downed
sycamore beside me in the murky
Blackstone appeared to me as the open arms
& spread, elevated legs of a nude
stretched out in the muddy riverbed,
than the suddenly clear blue sky reflected
in the dark water turned the river turquoise
& showed me where the life I've lost has flown.

Past is past. Downstream, all I could see
(or say) was *turquoise* then—the speechless earth
raised to the level, in a word, of heaven—
but I still mourned being left high & dry,
vis-à-vis the river, & insofar
as time has cut my water off down there.

*4. Record Temp*

Today I stretched my old legs in a fool's
paradise of sixty-five-degree weather
in early February, the Blackstone

at my side thawed in blister-spots & flowing
to the ocean audibly &, in places,
visibly. I'd broken out my all-seasons

turquoise North Face you got me for Xmas
but I was saving for the first spring day;
across the water, local ducks & geese

raised a ruckus, as if just as confused
as I was by the sudden change of climate
that set them off & saw me change my colors

to summer's, taking advantage of a glitch
in time to give my death march of days the slip.

*5. Timeline*

A great blue heron back another spring
tiptoed through last fall's leaves into the sun
& stood on one leg & then the other,
scratching its head with its free orange foot

on one side at a time, as if of two
minds about wading any deeper
into the whiskey-brown Blackstone Canal
I hugged its old towpath beside, following

in the footsteps of the oxen that long
ago towed barges loaded with cloth hot
off the loom from Slater Mill to the slate

Atlantic in the Bay. Every step I took
echoed their heavy steps that made history
& my feet here keep time with, to this day.

# AFTER LONG SILENCE

*for Emily*

Come a long way from riding her first wave,
down on all fours on her first board, to breaking
bread with me again, the dirty-blond
surfer back now like an epiphany

after ghosting me for almost a year,
tells me the best & brightest oysters hail
from dark water, cold & nearly black
with nutrients. The closest I will come

to surfing is catching a face-full of spray
while diving into an East Beach Blond all
liquor & pale flesh, then lapping up brine
& swallowing the sweet meat whole, washed down

with UFO White. Picking up today
where she left off, I can't believe my eyes.

## ORAL COMMUNICATION

*rose-rock, rose-quartz, roses, roses, roses,*
*exacting roses from the body . . .*
   ELIZABETH BISHOP

When she raised to my face her hand-held device
she kept cradled in her lap as though
reading her own palm, I came eye-to-eye

with her screen shot of a polished rose-quartz
as pink as the inside, say, of a conch shell—
the lodestone, in fact, of romantic love,

I learned from her. Sharing her resentment
that she felt forced to shave every last hair
on her body below the neck, she sent me
spiraling down it in imagination,

headfirst. I'd fallen for her the moment
I caught her staring at me as if reading
my lips & trying not to miss whatever
she might, by chance, have coming from my tongue.

## LOVE POEM TO MY FIRST READER

The racket in the air no longer came
from snow-blowers but from the early birds
staking out their territory again

another spring, the loudest of them all
our resident cardinal sounding off
with his exultant *pretty-pretty-pretty.*

Our dog raised his crescent-moon blond eyebrows
when I refused to let him out till that song
I'd waited all winter to hear once more

concluded. Bird-brained as I could be, I picked
up where it left off, & sang (so to speak)
of beauty, too—in truth, the common source

of love & poetry. O dearest figment
of my imagination to the end,
the world I lived in was a world imagined.

## JACK'S ABBY

Sycamores winter had stripped of their bark
down to their ghostly limbs underneath
crazed the sky, you said, "like white lightning"
on the first day of spring. Leaving the clinic

I had escaped with my life (thanks to you)
at the end of last spring, I got a clean bill
of health a year out & celebrated
with you when you kindly stopped at Jack's Abby

for his blood-orange wheat. You saw my fate
hang by a thread-thin wire (*pace* the Fates)
inside my pacemaker you had to green-light

my surgeon to bury in my chest, wary
of my "combative nature" as he said
he was, & get me started one last time.

## EASTER MONDAY

> *"Live all you can; it's a mistake not to."*
>     HENRY JAMES

Twenty years ago today I woke
in Paris & discovered the hard way
it was a holiday in France, each door
on every last street closed to me. I'd gone

hunting for the morning-after pill
even as the morning slipped away,
Plan B an option only in a drugstore
open in case of an emergency

such as I had on my hands then. I jumped
out of the cab I made the driver stop
in traffic when I spotted from his taxi
an open store I sprinted for through the rain,

as if my life, et cetera. It did,
in fact, just as my life was on the line
every single time I saw Paris, moved
to fly there as I always was by love.

# THE WHITE CROW

*(Rudolf Nureyev)*

Higher powers dressed him down for being
a "bad socialist," in love with all things
capitalist, because he wanted freedom
of self-expression & to be himself,
instead of tip-toeing the Party line.

He flew apart from the flock, as much alone
as I felt sitting at my private screening
of his life story in a theater
where flops go to die. In Paris he shopped

for a model of the Trans-Siberian
Express he was born on, but ended up
settling for the Orient Express
lost—his "Rosebud"—in his luggage sent
back East when he defected to the West.

# RACHMANINOFF'S "LILACS"

Every spring growing up in Minnesota,
I always heard if March came in (as now)
"like a lion" (snow everywhere & more
tonight), it would go out "like a lamb" (snow
nowhere to be found, snow-white though lambs are).
If that sounds like a problem, what about
lilacs that you can hear? Unheard-of, right?
I can't hear music, let alone lilacs,
but I still listen hard to it (as now).

I almost didn't graduate from college
when more than halfway through my final quarter
I stood to fail the last course that I needed
to pass (Music 101, as it happened).
Tone-deaf as I'd found out I was, I had
to face the music & squeeze a quarter-long
independent study of early modern
fiction into the time till graduation
when, in late spring, I stopped to smell the lilacs.

## OF LITTLE FAITH

My mother died when her replacement heart
valve hit its expiration date, & thirty
years later my own valve job proved the death
of me, when I saw the light—there is a there

*there*—& lived. Yet, back then, I'd sent her soul
into oblivion with my ungodly
words delivered, impromptu, in the presence
of her empty casket. I could only drive

my Alamo Horizon east from Disney
till the Beeline dead-ended in a tarred-
&-feathered beach near Cape Canaveral,

where I would launch her ashes into space
& she could watch, as she'd done from her yard,
shuttles blast off into eternity.

# IV

## SEEING DOUBLE IN NEW MEXICO

We are like night & day, the differences
between us evidenced in Albuquerque
when, gone shopping for summer clothes, you threw

up your hands & quit your search for tomorrow's
ideal cover-up, waving the white flag
of a blouse peppered with blue & red stars

visible as I came upon you like night
with stars of my own in hand, only white
sprinkled with red on a midnight-blue T.

After cruising past the manzanita,
sagebrush, & lavender to Santa Fe
in our Hertz Focus, I wondered suddenly

if all the Zuni fetishes there had lost
their edge, carved as a number of them were
from post-industrial waste like Technicolor

Fordite (badger), ruby-red gold slag (mole),
& sea-foam-shaded surfite (healing bear),
or had I lost my eye for them, as even

you feared? As different as we are, we still
saw eye to eye, whether we both had stars
in our eyes or both squinted hard together

into the future of our common love
of miniatures distilling the pure spirits
of untold animals that spoke to us

& we took home like rescues, missing parts
of ourselves whose call we both heard in our hearts—
two jet ravens, say, mirroring each other.

# MY FATHER CONTEMPLATES HIS
## HUNTING FETISH

After his second heart attack, he sat
in his gold chair at home in Golden Valley
& watched leaves turn outside our picture window

his last autumn. What hadn't changed? I'd gone
off to college, & our black Lab retriever
had to be put down. The only still poinr

remained his little blown-glass duck that sat
on my mother's prized mahogany end
table & glowed the amber of his nightly
Jim Beam on the rocks. There would be no more

sitting in a duck blind over a thermos
of her coffee spiked with bourbon at dawn
& waiting for the teal-wings to come in low
over the water, sitting ducks every time.

# NIGHT FLIGHT

At last I flew my private plane again
last night. Wings tipping left & right, my writing

hand gripped the joystick between my legs
as I tried staying on an even keel,

neither getting carried away nor losing
altitude. Without hard evidence

to the contrary, I'd given up hope
lately of taking flight, but there I sat

in mid-air suddenly, heart in my throat,
flying solo as I so often did

but never dreamed I would again, grounded
for life as I believed I'd been through no

failt of my own, till I got off the ground
in the dark one last time, white as a ghost.

B-17

A B-17 pinwheeled out of the sky
over Connecticut after a visit
to Quonset Point, critically injuring
three & killing seven. In the wake

of the war, I played with the model I built
of it, evading flak & Messerschmitts
over Germany as I imagined
flying it. Kenny Weinman, my father's friend

my mother called out as the handsomest
devil in Minneapolis (ever
dapper in a suit, dress shirt, & bowtie),
was small enough to serve as the tail-gunner

on it. He lived to hold his peace when asked
how many kills he had, & only said
to try & learn something new every day.
One day his wife, the beauty Emily,

found him, a diabetic, dead in bed.
Young as I was, I couldn't bear to think
of such a tough, sweet guy brought down by low
blood-sugar in the end. As a consequence,

I stand to crash & burn myself, resisting
going on the needle for fear of getting
caught, like him, without the Hershey bar
he carried with him when he came to visit.

## GLADIOLUS: A HISTORY

Taking home my first "Made in USA" glads
the "red-orange" of my favorite crayon
in school when I was little, I brought Nana

to life again in my mind. Labor Day,
when my parents drove us all across town
to Margaret & Art's to see my cousins,

we always had to stop at Lake of the Isles
& buy Nana a "flesh-pink" bunch of them,
her favorite flower & color (in my day).

She raised me my first two years of life,
the last two of the war, after my mother
went back to her office at Northern Pump,

a defense plant, & worked until ny father
sailed home from the South Pacific & laid
eyes on me at last. At night I ate holes,

moth-like, in Nana's nightgown the same pink
as those glads she held upright like a torch
lighting her way, as they did every last

summer's end, into the coming dark
I walk toward myself today, September
around the corner now with its deep shade.

## AGAINST WINTER

The crickets & the katydids still go
at it left & right, as I take my daily
walk under these trees while I still can:

the crickets plink out the higher notes
on a piano, & the katydids
hum along like powerlines in the wind

back where I come from. Yesterday you gave me
so many new turquoise gel pens I worry
I'll run out of days to use them all up.

Meanwhile, the white tip of a foraging
gray squirrel's tail flashing across my path
brings snow to mind before a leaf has fallen.

For the moment, though, I'll hot-foot it home
to you with a dozen tangerine roses.

## VARIABLE CLOUDINESS, THEN STARS

Last night you dreamed you were painting again,
something your day job keeps you from doing.
But in your sleep you turned your blank canvas
the artificial purple of grape soda
you discovered in the new Beauty Berries
now invading our yard in late November.

As for me, I stayed up for the duration
of what I knew, even then, had to be
a dream last night, & woke to yet another
loss today, when you drove me through a steady
downfall to a powwow on the coast,
hunting for my lost Native string of turquoise.

I asked a Narragansett elder for help
finding it; he just shook his head & sniffed,
"Southwest." Off in the gray-blue distance, surfers
black dots little bigger than eye-floaters
kept their heads above water & waited,
tied to their boards, for their wave to come in.

# PURSUING HAPPINESS

*for John*

1
After seeing our team's season unravel
this afternoon, my home-for-Xmas son
& I walked off our frustration half the length
of Benefit, the street where he was born
& raised that goes back to the Revolution.

I watched my step near sundown on the brick-
red cobblestones long underfoot & listened
as he translated for me what he'd heard
Turkish football fans chant in Trebizond:
"Those who follow their hearts take the heaviest fire"

—a sentence, as it happens, he has *lived:*
no toeing some company line at work,
no yes-man at home but an equal partner.
He's proved the free spirit I hoped he'd become.

2
I followed in the footsteps of my son
walking his mother halfway down the block
& back yesterday, with her on his arm

for support, along the very same path
she'd held his hand thirty-odd years in the past
on his first excursion away from home.

I watched their progress from the door. Tonight
he'll go to Boston & fly back from Xmas
to Istanbul, where she was born & his
troubles began two years ago, exactly,

when he got married. Whether he will follow
in my footsteps (divorce) remains to be seen
this record-breaking spring day in the middle
of January, two-faced as it is.

3
Thawing, the frozen river of my life
breaks into archipelagos of ice
floating on the surface of the water

streaming south to the sea, a jig-saw puzzle
gone to pieces before re-forming, like,
tomorrow. Meanwhile, cotton puffs of ducks

I've never seen before or will see again
have flown down from even farther north
& bob in the current, shunned as all six are
by a flock of local wood ducks as gray

as the woods I'm in. If my son were still here,
instead of back there on the other side
of the world, I'd tell him that the one constant
in it is change; his life depends on it.

# END OF STORY

A ghostly schematic of a Lancaster
bomber flies high above my kitchen,
hanging fire on the first day (& page)
of a new year (& calendar of vintage
early forties war planes roughly my age).

I was one when my Welsh grandfather John's
nephew hit Minneapolis with friends
on RAF R & R from Canada,
where they'd been shipped from England & got trained
to fly the plane I'm staring at, told

as I had been by everyone now gone
they'd taken turns launching me into the air,
leaving their fingerprints all over me,
the baby boy they'd never have themselves,
six months to live as they had to a man:

their Lancasters would get lost in the fog
or fall to friendly fire over the Channel
as they returned from bombing Germany,
finishing Hitler off to keep me free,
nobody there to catch them when they fell.

V

# WORLD WAR III

*1. The Daily News*

I will not live to see another spring
this year, killed as I must be by the latest
Chinese virus R & D'd in a lab

in Wuhan it escaped after a bat
infected with it accidentally
(or not) passed it on to a researcher

who, in turn, transmitted it to the public;
a million local carriers deployed
abroad for New Year's delivered it here.

The rest is history, including me
with my advanced age & diabetes,
which mean I top the list of those most likely

to fall in the onslaught. Even my death,
like too much in my life, was made in China.

*2. In Other News*

A woodpecker knocking on wood—*dead* wood,
it had to be, to house bugs—broke the stillness
along the river as I walked today
beside it on my once-daily escape

from quarantine. I kept my head down,
avoiding fellow POWs
taking a break, like me, from isolation
& checking their phones for news at every step.

I kept my distance, too, alone as I was
with my thoughts about where (or if) I'd be
buried. Staring at my feet, I exhibited

the shame already of a citizen
defeated in a war—with China, say,
in league with multinational elites.

*3. Report from Lincoln Woods*

I walked through the ghost town of the state park
I have as good as lived in twenty years.

Today the state declared it off-limits,
due to the Chinese-made virus recently

let loose on the world "accidentally
on purpose" (as I used to say as a kid).

Nukes launched by accident would trigger war;
instead, fallout from this event just meant

confining everyone to their own homes.
Gone AWOL for an hour, unmasked as I was,

I asked myself if all those empty campsites
previewed Memorial Day two months away

—if they remained abandoned (doctors' orders!)—
what would be left here worth remembering?

## 4. Park Closed on Account of Covid-19

No people crossed my path, but a yearling deer
the dusty tan of desert boots ignored
the six-feet rule of social distancing.

His or her herd, of course, had me outnumbered,
& I must have seemed on my way out, given
the sudden dearth of my kind thereabouts.

Illegal as my presence was today,
I dodged the State Police & found my way
to the man-made pond the heart of the park.

The first plane I had seen in weeks descended
over the water in such spooky silence
that I mistook it for a pterodactyl

or ventilators flying in from China
to profit from a global economy.

*5. Palm Sunday*

The Surgeon General warned the week ahead
would recall Pearl Harbor & 9/11—
sneak attacks, both, by foreign enemies—

& thus no different, to my mind (& maybe
his), from the Covid-19 attack,
except for its wear-&-tear on the social

fabric: bookstores, for instance, shuttered as "non-
essential." Since when? Without books, I mean,
where (or who) ever would I be now?

Bookstores attract the solitary, not
the crowds drawn to bars & restaurants,
so where's the harm (except to Amazon)

in letting them stay open? *Where have you gone,
Stillwater Books, small business big as life?*

6. *Among the Immortals*

You greeted me this morning with bad news
when there was nothing but: my boyhood idol,
Al Kaline, whose home jersey (#6)
hangs, signed & framed, in our living room,

died yesterday—one of so many taken
out of the blue I first saw him play under
at old Comiskey Park when I was twelve,
a visitor myself. I got to meet

my clean-cut hero there, after a game,
& two more times in Minneapolis;
I always found him kind & generous.

Tonight I'll see him in the afterlife,
reliving his star-turn in his one World
Series I'll watch again in black & white.

*7. Easter*

Every day I wake & take a deep breath
again is Easter, targeted for death
as my demographic is ("elderly,
with co-morbidties," chinks in the old

armour—Achilles' heels all). So I'm dying
to live to see these poems into print,
working against time to rise above it
in words that could outlast me in a book.

Daffodils come back to life today in time
for Easter recall the ear-pieces of two-
fisted, old-time, operator-assisted

crank phones, telling everyone quarantined
the good news safely, from such a distance
now as the law requires, if not belief.

8. *Observing Distance Breaking Quarantine*

The weather proved so beautiful today
I had no sooner started walking than
someone I failed to recognize but must
have known greeted me with my name (twice
the lawful distance away as she was).

*Hi, it's nice to see you!* I said & spent
most of my walk flipping through my mental
Rolodex (the only kind I've got)
of faces for her name. Then, within sight

of home, I heard a voice behind me praise
today's weather compared to yesterday's,
the only news available to us
poor lifeless souls who had met by accident,
before she passed (too close?) with her white poodle.

*9. Conversing with the Birds*

No sooner had I hoped to spot a red-
winged blackbird (my favorite as a kid)
in the wetlands below the covered bridge
I crossed into the park again today,

than a flash of red-orange caught my eye
like a spark risen from an unseen blaze
into the air but snuffed out in the green reeds
it dropped into in the blink of an eye.

It was a test whether the universe
answered my prayers whose age, et cetera,
the Chinese virus made a death sentence.

Then yesterday a great blue I felt blessed
to see flap out of prehistory here
hugged the water like its ancient spirit.

## 10. Under Lockdown

White as yesterday's mid-April snowfall,
a lone swan at Olney Pond socially
distancing or self-isolating gave me

pause, swimming along the shore of the marsh
connected to the pond at the park entrance
still closed officially to public access

until two weeks from now. For now he stuck
his bill into the fresh shoots to sniff out
newly hatched water-bugs to feed his family.

Making up his life story as I plodded
along, I got rebuffed by the blustery
wind off the pond. Whitecaps crowded its surface

like swans flocking together, free as birds
or as I could be, on penalty of death.

*11. Still Spring*

There comes a day in April here the trees
break into tiny leaves-to-be, each branch
outlined in green literally overnight.

Today's the day this year that takes my breath
away & shows me the white whale of Mrs.
Swan sitting on her eggs off in the distance,

beached on the sun-dried wetlands floor, her neck
signing her last initial on the air
like a vapor trail unwinding in the blue.

Speaking of blue, I get my son's screenshot
of four gem-like, genuinely turquoise eggs
a purple finch laid in a window-sill nest

at the old homestead. Birds look to the future
this spring; my future holds more house arrest.

*12. May Day*

Last night I dreamed a State Trooper stopped me
outside my house & said to stay inside,
reminding me the state remained locked down
till further notice. But then there I was, back

in the light of day, taking my daily walk
in the park under the *rat-a-tat-tat*
of a woodpecker bringing down the house
of bugs eating a tree out of house & home,

while peepers piped up for the first time
in a sweet spot of the woods suddenly
flooded by April showers. *A good sign!*

a fellow traveler & I agreed,
but not for us back at war with Red Chinese
now crossing borders far beyond the Yalu.

*13. Vespers in a Previous Life*

Twenty springs ago I stumbled on
the Cambridge University boys' choir
rehearsing in the chapel at Trinity

College for the Sunday morning service
one Saturday evening in early May
like this one here in *New* England, their voices

replaced by all manner of fly-by-night
birds chipping away with their chirps at the light
remaining. I never dreamed my high-flying

days would end with my being quarantined,
given my age & Type-2 diabetes,
on pain of death for good. No more freedom

of movement except for light exercise
in the yard, the prison yard, of my own home.

14. Vital Signs

*This is the kind of day I live for!* I heard
myself exclaim, when a blue jay swooped down
& landed at my feet like a chip off
the old sky still hanging over my head,
thank goodness, like all the leaf-lets on tree
after tree spreading the news of renewal
I hoped might rub off even on me.

Two chestnut horses rode out of Sunset
Stables, one small business back on its feet.
*Nobody listens to this governor!*
I overheard two park rangers agree
between themselves, as I left by the gate
& the guy fishing for his supper I'd asked,
*Any luck?* offered me a pond-caught trout.

*15. Swan Lake*

Yesterday I thought I was seeing things
swimming on the water—mouse-gray dust bunnies?—

between the swans in residence on Olney
Pond. Today I saw my mistake: two swan-lets

(*swanlings?*) close-flanked by their parents taking them
for an afternoon dip. So they've made good use

of this quiet time, following their nature
as I have followed mine, stringing these lines

together day by day to chronicle
living shut down, by decree, till whenever.

The lilacs in my yard have raised their plumes
of blue smoke, despite the air gone viral

("forever," on-air experts warn). Don't look now,
but life is taking back my neck of the woods.

*16. Double Feature*

I saw a woman bronzed & well-oiled wearing
a G-string & the mules supporting her
as she squatted down on her haunches & posed,
her back turned to an old man with a camera,
for soft-porn stills against the flattened pond.
They must have figured that the quarantine
guaranteed their privacy this morning,
in broad daylight & in the flesh. Back home,

I stumbled on an obviously lost
snapping turtle, big as a doll house
& weathered like a rock, dragging her long tail
through the grass in my yard. Her caramel eyes,
when I gazed into them, looked beyond me
down the road where she'd deposit her eggs.

*17. Evensong*

Bumblebees as big as hummingbirds plundered
the lavender wisteria in bloom
outside my door this morning as I ventured
forth another day, unmasked though I was

again, breathing the air at my own risk,
indefinitely fatal as it is
to my demographic alone (I'm told
by my jailers every day I'm locked down).

Glowing radioactive-green today,
every last tree in the woods takes a chance
on life (maybe its last, the way things look).

A junco in my honeysuckle here
warbles a song, unseen, into the evening,
telling his story one note at a time.

18. *Natural History*

Every day is a gift: right at the end
of my daily walk to & from the pond,
the family of swans residing there
turned up under my nose, swimming together

down a narrow inlet feeding the larger
body of water, & today the babies
were palpably *swans,* still gray in the shadow
of their mother but truly white in full sun.

Their father, teaching them the ropes of life
"at sea," snaked his neck out across the surface
for something invisible he tilted back

his head for & swallowed. He brought up the rear
when their mother paraded my way two blond
fuzz balls paddling their hearts out, all systems go.

*19. Memorial Day*

Known to the park staffers as "The Walker,"
according to my son's friend now a ranger,
I can't remember when the campsites here
were open last. Still closed today, they all

await an edict from on high before
their campfires can be lit, their smoke a signal
that one more summer has begun, but no
such memories are in the works this year.

Isn't this the outcome I feared, way back
when I began taking the pulse of being
endlessly quarantined? Meanwhile, my daily

excursions nowhere kept me sane, as I
held my breath & took steps toward the day
freedom goes viral, unmasked finally.

## 20. Under Attack

I saw my hometown (Stevens Avenue,
Lake Street) torched on live TV by outside
agitators—Red Blackshirts (Antifa)

hell-bent on burning down this country they learned
in school to hate & replace, piggy-backing
on anti-Blue protests, with Chinese-style

corporate communism. The governor here
showed health concerns didn't dictate her gag
order when, unmasked, she joined the mob paid
(my son reported to me from the scene)

for bombs thrown at squad cars. My rhododendrons
broke into a riot of ice-pink blooms
on my mother's birthday, viral kisses blown
into the air I can't breathe without loving.

www.ingramcontent.com/pod-product-compliance
Lightning Source LLC
Chambersburg PA
CBHW030345100526
44592CB00010B/837